E970.004 GAI   JUL   2007

GAINES, RICHARD M.

CHEROKEE
1577653777 $23.00 C2000

D0764551

Native Americans

The Cherokee

Richard M. Gaines

ABDO Publishing Company

visit us at
www.abdopub.com

Published by ABDO Publishing Company, 4940 Viking Drive, Suite 622, Edina, Minnesota 55435. Copyright © 2000 Abdo Consulting Group, Inc., Pentagon Tower, P.O. Box 36036, Minneapolis, Minnesota 55435 USA. International copyrights reserved in all countries. No part of this book may be reproduced in any form without written permission from the publisher.

Published 2000
Printed in the United States of America
Second printing 2002

Illustrator: David Kanietakeron Fadden
Cover & Interior Photos: Corbis
Editors: Bob Italia, Tamara L. Britton, Kate A. Furlong
Art Direction & Maps: Pat Laurel

Library of Congress Cataloging-in-Publication Data

Gaines, Richard M., 1942-
   The Cherokee/ Richard M. Gaines.
     p. cm. -- (Native Americans)
   Includes bibliographical references and index.
   Summary: Presents a brief introduction to the Cherokee Indians including information on their society, homes, food, clothing, crafts, and life today.
   ISBN 1-57765-377-7
   1. Cherokee Indians--Juvenile literature. [1. Cherokee Indians. 2. Indians of North America.] I. Title.

E99.C5 G14 2000
975'.0049755--dc21

99-059865

DRIFTWOOD PUBLIC LIBRARY
801 SW HWY 101
LINCOLN CITY OREGON 97367

Contributing Editor: Barbara A. Gray-Kanatiiosh, JD

Barbara Gray-Kanatiiosh, JD, is an Akwesasne Mohawk. She has a Juris Doctorate from Arizona State University, where she was one of the first recipients of ASU's special certificate in Indian Law. She is currently pursuing a Ph.D. in Justice Studies at ASU and is focusing on Native American issues. Barbara works hard to educate children about Native Americans through her writing and Web site where children may ask questions and receive a written response about the Haudenosaunee culture. The Web site is: www.peace4turtleisland.org

Illustrator: David Kanietakeron Fadden

David Kanietakeron Fadden is a member of the Akwesasne Mohawk Wolf Clan. His work has appeared in publications such as *Akwesasne Notes, Indian Time*, and the *Northeast Indian Quarterly*. Examples of his work have also appeared in various publications of the Six Nations Indian Museum in Onchiota, NY. His work has also appeared in "How The West Was Lost: Always The Enemy," produced by Gannett Production which appeared on the Discovery Channel. David's work has been exhibited in Albany, NY; the Lake Placid Center for the Arts; Centre Strathearn in Montreal, Quebec; North Country Community College in Saranac Lake, NY; Paul Smith's College in Paul Smiths, NY; and at the Unison Arts & Learning Center in New Paltz, NY.

Contents

Where They Lived

For a thousand years before Christopher Columbus discovered America, the Cherokee lived in the Appalachian Mountains. This area is in present-day Tennessee, Virginia, Kentucky, North Carolina, South Carolina, Georgia, and Alabama.

The Cherokee homelands had low mountains covered with hardwood forests. The forests were full of deer, turkey, bear, and other game. The streams and rivers were full of fish.

The land of the Cherokee

Cherokee homelands also had many caves. In fact, the word *Cherokee* means "the tribe of the caves" in Choctaw. But, the Cherokee call themselves "Ani'-yun' wiya," which means "The People." They watched over the earth and protected it.

The Cherokee Homelands

Society

The Cherokee lived in villages along streams and rivers. Often, each village had several hundred homes. It also had its own **council** and chiefs.

In the center of the village was a large, round council house and a public square. There, the members of the seven Cherokee **clans** discussed important matters. The government was a **democracy**. It was based on people being equal.

The **clan** system was important to Cherokee society. The seven Cherokee clans are Wolf, Deer, Bird, Paint, Longhair, Blue, and Wild Potato. These clans connect the people to nature. They also make the Cherokee one large family.

The Cherokee society had no police. Their laws were based on **traditional** teachings. Families sought justice for any wrongs committed against their members.

In the late summer or early fall, the Cherokee hold the Green Corn Ceremony. It gives thanks for the harvest. And, it renews the balance between the Cherokee and the natural world.

The ceremony begins at dawn. During the day, people give speeches that tell the Cherokee history. People also play games, sing songs, and perform dances. There is a great feast, too.

A Cherokee village

Homes

The Cherokee lived in circular homes made from poles, sapling trees, mud, and **wattle** mats. The mud and wattle homes were warm in the winter and cool in the summer.

The Cherokee made wattle mats by weaving together sticks and reeds. Then, they attached the mats to the poles and saplings that formed the home's frame. To finish the house, the Cherokee covered the mats with mud.

The Cherokee covered the roof with thatch. A hole in its center let out the smoke from the fire pit inside.

The Cherokee slept on boughs piled on the ground. Later, they put up benches along the wall. They used the benches as sleeping platforms and tables.

In the eighteenth century, European traders introduced metal tools to the Cherokee. Some Cherokee used the new tools to build log cabins instead of their **traditional** homes.

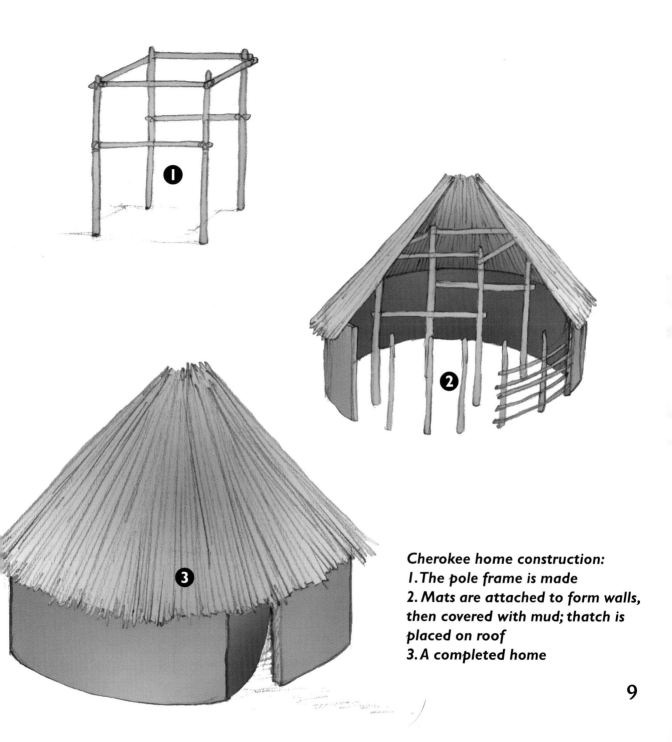

Cherokee home construction:
1. The pole frame is made
2. Mats are attached to form walls, then covered with mud; thatch is placed on roof
3. A completed home

9

Food

The Cherokee planted gardens with corn, squash, beans, potatoes, melons, and pumpkins. Women gathered berries, fruits, and nuts from the forest. They also picked greens and herbs from the fields for food and medicine.

Cherokee darts

The men hunted bear, turkey, and deer with bows and arrows. Small animals, like game birds, were hunted with a blow gun. A blow gun is a tube-shaped weapon with a dart inside. The hunter launches the dart by blowing into the tube.

The Cherokee made blow guns from river cane. They were about six feet (1.8 m) long. The darts were made from locust wood. The Cherokee attached **down** from the thistle plant to one end of the dart. This made the dart fly straight.

Deer were important to the Cherokee. They used almost every part of the animal. The Cherokee ate the meat. They **tanned** the hides to make leather moccasins and clothes. They made glue from the hooves and thread from the **sinew**. They made tools, needles, and ornaments from the bones.

The Cherokee fished with hooks carved from bone. They also caught fish with spears, bows and arrows, traps, and handwoven nets made from plant fibers.

The **traditional** teachings taught the Cherokee to maintain balance with the natural world. So, the Cherokee were careful not to kill more animals or plants than they needed to survive.

A Cherokee man catches fish by chasing them with arrows into a trap.

Clothing

The Cherokee homelands had hot, sticky summers. So, they wore little clothing. Men and boys wore only **breechcloths** and moccasins. Women and girls wore only a skirt wrapped around their waists. Young children wore no clothes at all.

In the cold winters, men wore buckskin leggings and shirts. Women wore soft, white skirts and dresses made from deerskin. Both men and women wore fur robes to keep warm. They also wore jewelry made of bone, shell, and beads.

After the Europeans arrived in America, the Cherokee traded for goods such as brass kettles, blankets, and cloth. One type of trade cloth was calico. It is made from cotton. Calico cloth has a solid background with designs of tiny flowers, leaves, or vines.

Cherokee women used calico cloth to make long blouses and skirts. Today, this style of dress is known as a "tear dress." Many believe the name of the dress came from the way the women had to cut the cloth by tearing it.

Men wrapped calico around their head like a **turban**. During war, the Cherokee men wore deer tails and white feathers on their turbans. They did this so they could tell the difference between themselves and other Native Americans during battle.

A Cherokee family in traditional clothing

Crafts

Cherokee men made dugout canoes. First, they carefully selected a tulip poplar tree with a large, straight trunk. The Cherokee said a prayer to thank the tree for giving up its life. Then, the Cherokee set a small fire at the tree's base to cut it down.

The men took the tree trunk back to the village and removed the bark. They carved the outside of the trunk into a canoe shape. Then, they hollowed out the trunk with fire.

After the canoe was hollowed out and shaped, the men painted it. The Cherokee used natural paints made from plants, barks, and clay. Making a canoe took much skill, work, and patience.

Cherokee women created beautiful baskets from river cane and white oak. Today, baskets are also made from honeysuckle. At one time, baskets were necessary for survival. But now, they are mostly an art form.

Splint baskets were make from white oak trees. The trees were chosen carefully. After being cut down, the tree was placed on wooden stands and flattened with a blunt stone axe.

After being pounded, the tree separated into splints along its year rings. Before the women made a basket, they had to cut the splints to the size needed. Some splints were left their natural wood color. Other splints were dyed.

The women soaked the splints in water to make them soft. Then, they wove the splints into a basket. The baskets were round or rectangular.

A Cherokee woman weaving splint baskets

Family

Cherokee marriage ceremonies were brief and simple. The bride and groom met at the council house. The groom gave the bride a venison ham. The bride gave the groom an ear of corn. After the offering of gifts, the ceremony continued with a great feast and dance.

The new couple lived with the wife's family. Her family included her mother, her married sisters and their families, and her unmarried brothers.

If the husband and the wife **divorced**, the wife and her children remained in the mother's family. The divorced husband returned to his mother's family. He lived there until he married again.

In Cherokee society, the children belong to the mother's **clan**. Clans are very important. Women and men cannot marry a person from their clan. This is because clan members are considered one family.

A Cherokee marriage ceremony

Children

Fathers taught their boys how to hunt and fish. A strong friendship existed between father and son for their entire lives.

The most important men in a boy's life were his uncles. An uncle decided when the boy was old enough to go to war and help make family decisions.

The women taught Cherokee girls all of the home and gardening skills. Cherokee children were never spanked. But, the family elders teased them if they misbehaved.

Next page: A Cherokee father teaches his son how to track an animal.

Myths

The Cherokee believed the sky was made of solid rock. The earth was an island, which hung from the sky by four ropes.

The Cherokee believed they descended from the first man, Kanati, and the first woman, Selu.

When Kanati needed food, he went into the swamp. Kanati made arrows for his hunt. He picked strong reeds and fit feathers to one end and a flint arrowhead to the other end.

After making his arrows, Kanati went into the woodlands to a place where a giant rock stood. He pushed the rock to one side. Out from an underground cave came a deer or other game. He killed the animal instantly with one arrow. This is how Kanati hunted.

Selu took a large basket and went to a building where the food was stored. Once inside, she rubbed her stomach and the basket became almost filled with corn. When she rubbed her legs, the basket filled the rest of the way with beans.

Selu prepared the corns and beans to eat. She made many types of dishes. She made corn mush and cornbread with beans.

When Selu died, she was buried. On top of her grave grew corns and beans. This is why the Cherokee say men became hunters, and the women tended the homes and gardens.

The Cherokee believed Kanati (left) and Selu were the first man and woman.

War

The Cherokee went to war to **avenge** the death of relatives. The spirits of the dead family members could not rest until their families avenged the crime.

The entire village had to agree to go to war. War parties usually consisted of 20 to 30 men and one woman. She was called the war woman. She watched the captives, and she cooked for the entire party. When the war party killed the same number of enemies as had been killed in the Cherokee village, they went home.

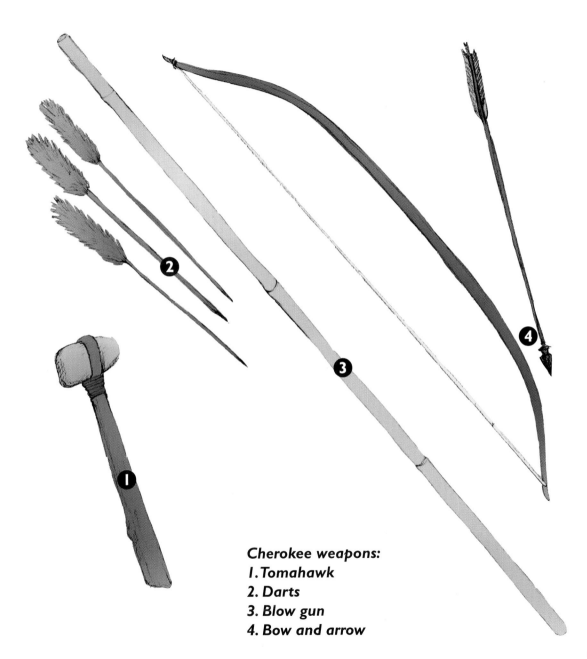

Cherokee weapons:
1. Tomahawk
2. Darts
3. Blow gun
4. Bow and arrow

Contact with Europeans

The Cherokee first met Europeans in 1540. That's when Spanish explorer Hernando de Soto and his men reached the Cherokee homelands in South Carolina and Georgia. De Soto was looking for gold. Sadly, the Europeans brought diseases that killed many Cherokees.

Later, the Cherokees signed **treaties** with the British. Some of the Cherokee chiefs went to England to meet royalty. The Cherokee and British fought the American **colonists** in the Revolutionary War.

In 1814, the Cherokee helped Andrew Jackson and the U.S. Army to defeat the Creek Red Sticks. The Cherokee lost more men in the battle than the army.

Soon after Andrew Jackson became U.S. president, he made war on the Cherokee. In 1830, President Jackson proposed the Indian Removal Bill in the U.S. **Congress**. The bill became law.

The law allowed the U.S. to remove the Cherokee and other Native Americans from their **traditional** homelands so whites could settle in the area. Cherokee homes were burned. Their possessions were stolen.

The men, women, and children were marched by force toward present-day Oklahoma. Sometimes, families were separated. Only the sick and elderly could ride on wagons. Everyone else had to walk. There was little food or clean water.

More than 4,000 Cherokee died during the 116-day march. The dead were buried along the side of the trail. Leaving their homelands and losing people along the way made them cry. This 800-mile (1,287-km) march to Oklahoma is known today as the Trail of Tears.

A nineteenth century oil painting of the Trail of Tears

Sequoyah

Sequoyah (Sik-wa-yi) was born around 1770. His mother was Cherokee. Her family came from a long line of chiefs.

When Sequoyah became an adult, he took the name of George Guess. The name came from an American trader whom Sequoyah believed was his father.

In 1820, Sequoyah overheard two men speaking. They talked about how white men could read marks on paper. These marks carried the voice of men a great distance. Sequoyah became interested in these "talking papers."

Sequoyah believed the Cherokee language could also be written. He began to create a picture symbol for each word in his language. Sequoyah spent much time working on these symbols. His wife, Sally, thought he was doing **witchcraft**. So, she burned down their house. All of his work was destroyed.

Sequoyah was not mad. He realized there were too many pictures to draw and to remember. He had a better idea.

Sequoyah listened to the sounds of the Cherokee language. Then he created a mark for each of the sounds.

Sequoyah holding the Cherokee alphabet

Sequoyah's Cherokee alphabet has **86** letters. His first student was his six-year-old daughter. She learned to read and write the Cherokee language from her father's alphabet.

In 1821, Sequoyah and his daughter wrote and read messages from each other using the Cherokee alphabet. This convinced the Cherokee people that the "talking papers" were not **witchcraft**. They realized how important it was to communicate in writing.

The alphabet was easy to learn. The Cherokee learned it quickly. Soon, there was a Cherokee newspaper and books.

President James Monroe invited Sequoyah to Washington, D.C. Monroe gave Sequoyah a medal for his great accomplishment.

Sequoyah died in 1843. He will always be remembered for inventing the Cherokee alphabet.

The Cherokee Today

The Indian Removal Bill and the Trail of Tears were hard on the Cherokee people. Even with such difficulties, the Cherokee and their **culture** have survived.

Some Cherokee were able to reclaim land in their **traditional** homelands in North Carolina. Some have made Oklahoma their new home. Many people became scattered throughout the world. These people are now trying to find their way back to their Cherokee roots.

Today, there are three Cherokee **reservations**: The Eastern Band of Cherokee Indians of North Carolina, the Cherokee Nation of Oklahoma, and the United Keetoowah Band of Cherokee Indians of Oklahoma.

The Cherokee Nation and United Keetoowah Band in Oklahoma have more than 115,000 members. The Eastern Band of Cherokee in North Carolina has more than 12,500 members.

The Eastern Band of Cherokee Indians has **cultural** programs that are open to the public. One program, the Oconaluftee Indian Village in Cherokee, North Carolina, can be visited from May 15 though October 25.

Oconaluftee is a re-creation of an eighteenth century Cherokee village. Guides tell about Cherokee history and culture. Cherokee people are dressed in **traditional** clothing. There are men making dugout canoes and **knapping** flint. You'll also find women doing beadwork, making baskets and pottery, and weaving belts.

Knapping flint

Weaving a belt

Making pottery

Another public program is a play called *Unto These Hills*. The outdoor theater is near the Oconaluftee Indian Village. The play tells the history of the Cherokee from de Soto's arrival in 1540 to the Trail of Tears in 1838. The play has 130 actors. *Unto These Hills* can be seen from mid-June to August at the Eastern Band of Cherokee Indian **Reservation** in North Carolina.

Each year, Cherokee ceremonial dancers participate in the Chehaw National Indian Festival in Chehaw Park, Albany, Georgia.

A cherokee ceremonial dancer

cherokee in a dance competition

Glossary

avenge - to seek revenge for something.

breechcloth - a length of leather or cloth that goes between a man's legs and is held up by a belt around his waist.

clan - a group of families that were related through their mother's line. This is true for many Native Americans. But, some tribes trace clans on both their mother and father's sides.

colonist - a person who lives in a colony; a settler.

Congress - the national lawmaking body of the United States.

council - a group of people who meet, usually to make decisions.

culture - the customs, arts, and tools of a nation or people at a certain time.

democracy - a government run by the people who live under it.

divorce - the legal ending of a marriage.

down - any fine, soft hair or fuzz.

knap - to shape by breaking off pieces.

reservation - land set aside by the government for a special purpose.

sinew - tendon, the tissue that connects a muscle to bone.

tan - to make a hide into leather by soaking it in a special liquid.

tradition - the handing down of beliefs, customs, and stories from parents to children.

treaty - a formal agreement, especially one between nations, signed and approved by each nation.

turban - a scarf wound around the head or around a cap.

wattle - sticks and branches woven together.

witchcraft - what a witch does or is believed to be able to do; magic power.

Web Sites

The official site of the Eastern Band of Cherokee: **http://www.cherokee-nc.com/**

The official site of the Cherokee Nation of Oklahoma: **http://www.cherokee.org/**

Oconaluftee Indian Village: **http://www.dnet.net/~cheratt**

For information on the National Museum of the American Indian, see the Smithsonian's Web site at **http://www.si.edu/organiza/museums/amerind/abmus/index.htm**

These sites are subject to change. Go to your favorite search engine and type in "Cherokee" for more sites.

Index